contents

INTRO

People who work in the field of digital media create the video, animation, graphics, text, and other elements used for a variety of applications, from entertainment to scientific research.

Published in 2018 by The Rosen Publishing Group, Inc.
29 East 21st Street, New York, NY 10010

Copyright © 2018 by The Rosen Publishing Group, Inc.

First Edition

All rights reserved. No part of this book may be reproduced in any form without permission in writing from the publisher, except by a reviewer.

Library of Congress Cataloging-in-Publication Data

Names: Brezina, Corona, author.
Title: Careers in digital media / Corona Brezina.
Description: New York : Rosen Publishing Group, Inc., 2018 | Series: Essential careers | Includes bibliographical references and index. | Audience: Grades 7–12.
Identifiers: LCCN 2017015803 | ISBN 9781538381526 (library bound) | ISBN 9781508178743 (paperback)
Subjects: LCSH: Digital media—Vocational guidance—Juvenile literature. | Multimedia systems—Vocational guidance—Juvenile literature.
Classification: LCC QA76.575 .B745 2018 | DDC 006.7023—dc23
LC record available at https://lccn.loc.gov/2017015803

Manufactured in China

19-0129
WILLIMANTIC PUBLIC LIBRARY
CHILDREN'S DEPARTMENT

essential careers™

CAREERS IN
DIGITAL MEDIA

VHKJ79DSG7DR56YG

CORONA BREZINA

Rosen
YA

New York

DUCTION

Professionals in the field of digital media follow a diverse range of career paths. They work as graphic designers in advertising, web designers creating web pages, writers maintaining blogs, and much more. Regardless of specialization, they all have one factor in common. When they get to their job in the morning, they'll probably sit down at a computer to start work. By definition, digital media is content read and transmitted by computers and other devices. Many jobs in digital media involve a high degree of creativity, but they also require technical competence using computer software.

Another common factor is that most people working in digital media are creating content for an audience. Their public may be movie fans, gamers, readers, TV viewers, people browsing the web, smartphone users, or potential customers for a product in an ad or social media marketing campaign.

Luckily for experts in digital media, the audience for digital media is enthusiastic and growing. In the distant past, people were restricted to watching moving pictures exclusively in movie theaters. Options were limited for people who wanted to read news articles as well—they generally had to buy their own paper copy of a newspaper or magazine. The advent of television increased the amount of media programming made available to the public, but people still generally watched TV at home on big immobile screens. Today, such limitations to consuming media have largely been eliminated. More and more people are acquiring smartphones and other mobile devices that provide a seemingly infinite supply of media of all varieties—words, images, and videos in every combination. For professionals who work in fields related to digital media, this insatiable appetite for digital media represents a vast audience for their creations.

The existence of a potential audience doesn't guarantee success, however. People in digital media have to understand and engage their audience. They work long hours to produce movies that will become box office hits, games that keep users enthralled day after day, blogs that fans check regularly for updates, and successful campaigns in advertising, marketing, or social media that make customers excited about a product or service.

To capture an audience, the people involved in creating digital media content have to be fans of the medium themselves. They have to be passionate about movies, TV shows, games, online prose, and social media interactions. Just about everyone enjoys passive consumption of various forms of digital media. But are you someone whose interest goes beyond mild appreciation? Does an action-packed movie, game, or stylish web page make you say, "I wish I could do something like that!" or even, "I could do better than that!"? If so, you might consider looking into a career in digital media.

chapter 1

EXPLORING THE FIELD OF DIGITAL MEDIA

Digital media is all pervasive in the modern world, even though the term "digital media" itself might make you think of the high-tech exhibits in museums or cutting-edge special effects in movies. You might not immediately consider the various forms of digital media that most ordinary people experience in their everyday lives. Digital media is in your music, is displayed on ads that catch your eye in public spaces, and makes up the content on your mobile devices, computers, and TVs. It's very likely that you use digital media at school and work and unwind with different forms of digital media at the end of the day.

Digital media has transformed many industries and created new niches for experts in the field who possess both technical expertise and a creative flair. Even the job description of "digital media specialist" is a relatively new idea—not long ago, in the late 1990s, social media didn't exist, internet commerce was a small market, and high-quality videos and animations could be produced only by big companies. Since then, technology has advanced, and all three of these elements are part of the routine in the daily work of a digital media specialist.

Educational digital media is increasingly being incorporated into the classroom, expanding the range of instructional resources and high-tech activities available to students.

WHAT IS DIGITAL MEDIA?

At its most basic, digital media is encoded content that is read and transmitted by computers and other devices. This encoded content includes text, audio, video, and image files. These basic building blocks are combined to create the music, films, video games, websites, and other forms of information and entertainment that most people access every day in multiple forms.

The rise of digital media massively disrupted the traditional media industry. Newspapers suffered, for example, as they lost advertising revenue and readership to online competitors. Nevertheless, digital media offers exciting opportunities to imaginative, tech-savvy individuals interested in creating, developing, editing, and publicizing digital media content.

Some businesses and organizations employ digital media specialists to manage all their digital media requirements. These specialists are responsible for the design and maintenance of the company's web page as well as blogging, creating and uploading videos, and managing its social media presence. By contrast, many people who work in digital media specialize in a particular area. Are you a video game fanatic? Do you love cartoons and other forms of

A cartoonist at the Ankama studio in France sketches a character, Dofus, on his computer. The popular video game character is being adapted into a film.

animations? Do you find yourself admiring the graphic design of images and layouts? Are the special effects your favorite parts of movies? Do you sometimes find yourself thinking, "I could write a better story than this" when reading online content? Are you drawn to computer programming and the potential to improve the software used in manipulating digital media? Have you ever designed your own website for fun in your spare time? If you see yourself in any of these descriptions, you might think about pursuing a future career related to digital media.

OUTLOOK FOR CAREERS IN DIGITAL MEDIA

Up-to-date data on long-term outlook and salary for careers of all types can be accessed in the *Occupational Outlook Handbook* (*OOH*) created by the Bureau of Labor Statistics (BLS), an agency within the US Department of Labor. The *OOH* is a good starting point if you're researching a range of careers related to digital media.

Many of the specializations within the field of digital media are listed under the classification of Multimedia Artists and Animators.

DIGITAL MEDIA AND LEARNING

Many of the careers most associated with digital media fall within fields such as entertainment, technology, marketing, and advertising. But digital media is also transforming how children learn and experience the world. Today, digital media is highly relevant to teachers and other professionals in education. At its best, digital media can engage students through technology-enabled classrooms and resources on personal tablets or laptops. But some parents and educators worry that excessive digital media use could impact the development of thinking and social skills. If you have a passion for digital media and education, consider career opportunities that combine both interests. You could incorporate the latest digital media tools into your own lesson plans as a teacher or consider jobs in education administration, research, or specialized areas such as digital learning or instructional technology.

This occupation category includes the digital media specialists who are responsible for animation and special effects in media such as TV, movies, and video games. Some of the other specializations can be found under categories such as media and communication, computer and information technology, and arts and design.

There's a growing consumer demand for digital media, especially for types involving animation and visual effects. This trend is reflected in the outlook for occupations related to digital media. Employment in most of these occupations is expected to grow, some at a faster than average rate. Most careers in digital media pay above average—up-to-date figures can be accessed in the *OOH*.

Aspiring digital media specialists should expect to complete extensive education and training before they enter the workforce. Most digital

Animators work in many different applications in digital media. They often specialize in a certain type of production or a specific niche, such as designing background landscapes for games.

media occupations require a bachelor's degree for an entry level job. Possible college majors include art, communications, journalism, film, broadcasting, animation, graphic design, computer science, programming, web design, or computer graphics. Some colleges do offer a major in digital media.

A range of different types of companies employ people who specialize in various types of digital media. These include employers in the motion picture and video industries, computer software companies, graphic design studios, advertising agencies, broadcasting, and the publishing industry. You might end up working in an office or computer lab of a big company; other digital media specialists work in mid-size firms or start-ups. Some digital media specialists work freelance and decide their own work environment and schedule. Regardless, you should anticipate long hours sitting at a computer if you pursue a career in digital media.

WORKING AS A DIGITAL MEDIA SPECIALIST

Many employers hire digital media specialists to oversee their media presence as it's experienced by customers or by an audience. The digital media specialist may work closely with the marketing department to promote the company's brand identity. A digital media specialist's day-to-day tasks vary depending on the company's needs. A digital media specialist working for a retailer, for example, may focus primarily on social media interactions that promote the company's products. Someone working for a TV station might be responsible for producing and uploading text, video, and

Jobs in digital media require proficiency in a variety of software and web tools, but expertise in shooting photos and videos can also be an attractive asset to employers.

audio content, along with managing the web design and graphic design. A digital media specialist should be comfortable with creating and managing all forms of digital media.

The job requires technical know-how as well as creativity and strong communication skills. A digital media specialist must be proficient in a variety of different software tools used in media production, web design, and marketing and also be familiar with various social media platforms. Some positions involve shooting video, in which case the digital media specialist must be able to operate video production equipment.

The digital media specialist needs to have excellent verbal, presentation, and social media communication skills—the person in this position often coordinates closely with other departments in the company and interacts with the public. Writing and editorial skills, with an ability to pay close attention to detail, are also important, as are organizational and time-management skills.

A digital media specialist also needs to address the creative requirements of the job. He or she is responsible for producing effective, visually appealing, and persuasive content. Images and videos should grab the viewer's attention, and websites should be engaging and easy to navigate. Employers will look for candidates who can bring fresh ideas to the company.

chapter 2

CAREER PATHS IN DIGITAL MEDIA

Most professionals who work in digital media specialize in a specific area of the field. They're responsible for the content, appearance, and sounds of digital media products of all kinds. These specialists create or edit digital effects, audio, images, interactive features, and text in movies, TV shows, animated clips on the internet, and video games. They work for big studios and media companies and smaller firms that provide digital media services in specific niches. Many work freelance, signing up for projects with a range of employers. Digital media jobs can be demanding, requiring long hours, but digital media professionals consider the rewards of the field to be worth the hard work. The following are descriptions of some of the related career paths in digital media.

DIGITAL EDITOR

Digital editors, video editors, and film editors organize raw footage into a completed movie, TV episode, news clip, advertisement, or other form of media. For a big project such as a film or documentary, editing is a major undertaking that involves cutting, selecting, arranging, and splicing together scenes from the huge amount of material shot by the camera

A digital editor reviews files during the process of putting together the individual shots, scenes, special effects, music, and other elements that ultimately make up the final product.

crew from multiple angles. The different versions put together during the process are called cuts. The end result that reaches the audience is called the final cut.

Even though digital editing is a postproduction process—meaning, after the footage has been shot—the digital editor begins work during the preproduction stages by reading the script and making suggestions that are taken into account when scheduling the shooting. He or she reviews footage after each day of shooting.

Digital editing requires both a broad creative vision and close attention to detail. Digital editors take many factors into account in making choices about what shots to include in each scene. Depending on the type of media, the final result is expected to tell a story, create a riveting choreographed spectacle, or inform and educate the audience. Effective pacing is crucial for a successful final cut. The digital editor may also have to consider factors such as cinematography, timing, and character development. Sometimes, the digital editor has to compensate for shortcomings in the footage or correct for color.

TIPS FROM THE PROS

Shane Ross, freelance film editor

"I … like the fact that I work on a variety of show types. From scripted shows to documentary shows, to reality, to show pitches. I haven't been pigeon holed into one category. This also means that I'm constantly learning and constantly developing new and creative editing techniques …

- I dislike the hours. I work 10 hours a day, five days a week, sometimes six. And sometimes I'm required to work late.
- The one thing that was very often asked for after I left college was a 'demo reel,' a sample of your work.
- Network, and by that I mean just meet and talk to other editors, other people in your field. Just knowing someone and being personable can get you your first big break.
- Here's a good one: Watch a LOT of movies and TV, things you are wanting to work on."

(Source: The Art Center Project. "How to Become a Film Editor." Retrieved March 9, 2017. http://www.theartcareerproject.com /become-film-editor.)

The digital editor works closely with the director, with the sound and music editors, and with other members of the editing team. At other times, the editor spends long hours working alone at the computer editing footage using various types of software.

VISUAL EFFECTS PRODUCER

Visual effects producers, visual effects supervisors, artists, and technicians use computer software to create the special effects seen in movies, TV shows, and other forms of video. Visual effects producers create spectacular scenes that could not occur in real life through computer-generated imagery (CGI), but they also manipulate small details to add aesthetic appeal, increase the drama of a scene, or simply fix mistakes.

Visual effects are added postproduction. But visual effects producers work with the director and producer for a project from the preproduction stage. The visual effects producer begins by reading the script and compiling a list of necessary visual effects, along with the cost. The visual effects team then plans how to create each effect and draws up a schedule. Some special effects are performed on set while others are exclusively digital; sequences can also be combinations.

Visual effects producers must be creative, technologically adept, and detail oriented. Effects must mesh perfectly with the other elements of a scene. A technician or artist may specialize in a particular technique. For example, specialists called compositors combine layers of different types of video material to create the final image, while other visual effects technicians edit special effects footage to create a clean and coherent final product.

SOUND DESIGNER

The sound designer is responsible for the sound effects heard in movies, TV shows, video games, and other forms of media. The sound designer often joins the project in the preproduction stage and plans the overall tone and the variety of sounds that will be heard through the final result. The sound designer may invent sound combinations to accompany special effects, such as a roaring monster or a huge explosion. He or she also adds spot effects that match action and background atmosphere sounds.

Many sound designers also work as sound editors or sound mixers, who record sounds during shooting and adjust the final balance of sound elements. Postproduction, sound designers digitally edit the sounds, experimenting with and adjusting various elements. They might filter out unwanted noise or rere-cord and replace certain sounds. Some sound designers may be involved in editing the music and combining all the sound elements in the final track.

A sound designer should be experienced in recording, editing, and mixing sound, including proficiency in various types of software used in the industry. Many sound designers have a background in music. A sound designer should also have a firm understanding of acoustics—how sound is transmitted within a space—as well as psychoacoustics, which deals with human perception of sound.

GRAPHIC DESIGNER

Graphic designers—sometimes called graphic artists or communication designers—create the design elements that make up any type of media intended to have a visual impact. Traditionally, these have included print applications such as posters, book covers, and the graphics in newspapers and magazines. Many advertising agencies employ graphic designers to design eye-catching displays. Businesses hire graphic designers to create promotional materials and logos that will be instantly recognizable to consumers. Even as technology evolves, graphic designers are still in demand to create content for new forms of media, such as TV graphics, images on websites, software design, and icons for mobile devices. They also work on content for video games, movies, and animation.

Graphic designers develop the images and work on the appearance of the text and the overall layout for a project. They combine these elements and use color choices to grab the viewer's attention or convey a message. Most graphic designers work using computer software, although they may create designs by hand, too. Graphic designers sometimes work as part of a team,

Graphic designers, who are responsible for visual elements such as layout, images, and text in a variety of media, aim to make an impression on viewers or get across an idea or concept.

and they may collaborate closely with other specialists involved in the content or concepts for a project, such as writers or people from the marketing department of a company.

3D ARTIST

Three-dimensional (3D) artists, along with the 3D designers and 3D modelers, create 3D graphics and animations used in a variety of media. Three-dimensional elements have become prevalent in many forms of entertainment, such as movies, cartoons, video games, TV shows, and websites, but they are also valuable in various fields of science, medicine, engineering, architecture, and advertising.

All 3D artists use software to create digital models and then fill in the visual details, although sometimes they produce illustrations by hand or build physical models as part of the process. As is the case with many other digital media jobs, 3D art and animation require both artistic and technical ability. Some 3D artists start out as animators or video game artists before developing an expertise in 3D work. Many 3D artists work in a team and cooperate closely with directors, writers, designers, and others involved in a project. Generally, 3D artists specialize in a specific design category, such as characters or background scenery.

DIGITAL ANIMATOR

Digital animators produce moving images using computer software. Today, potential jobs for animators extend far beyond creating cartoon entertainment for children. Animators produce many of the visual effects in action movies, on websites, and in video games. Animation isn't exclusively created for entertainment, either. Forensic animators re-create crime scenarios, for example, while medical animators portray medical devices or procedures.

An animator may work on projects as part of a team for large projects or produce smaller animation sequences independently. Some animators specialize in a particular aspect of animation; these niches can overlap with those of 3D artists. An animator may work mainly on background, layout, texture of different elements in the animation, or lighting.

Animators must have strong artistic abilities. Digital animators often also possess drawing and traditional animation skills in addition to digital proficiency. Animators must have an astute understanding of how figures move, and they tend to observe the

TIPS FROM THE PROS

Rebecca Perez, animator

- "I would consider myself a general artist turned animator. I love all aspects of art such as sculpting, 3d modeling, painting, storytelling, photography and of course animation.
- My very first job was as a '3D Technical Artist' at Lucasarts. I had just graduated from Ringling [School of Art and Design] and to be quite honest, I just wanted to get my foot in the door … It helped me connect with other animators and gave me production experience that I needed.
- Master the Principles of Animation. Be humble and ask questions. Learn how to create and give a sincere performance in your animation. Be flexible and able to adapt to change. Learn how to manage your time. And lastly have a positive attitude!"

(Source: Milton, Dell. "Dreamworks Animator Rebecca Perez." Animation Area. Retrieved March 9, 2017. http://www .animationarena.com/dreamworks-animator-rebecca-perez.html.)

world around them with an eye for movement and expression. A career in animation may require long hours with tight deadlines, but most animators love their jobs—they often report that at the end of the day, they work on independent projects for fun and unwind with various forms of animated media.

VIDEO GAME DESIGNER

The video game designer is responsible for the vision and development of video games. Many of the previous careers, such as sound designers and animators, can be found across a broad range of different types of digital media. By contrast, the video game designer's job is specific to the industry. Many aspects of video game creation, such as devising rules for the game, assessing the user's experience, and working within the limitations of various hardware platforms, don't have any exact parallel in movie and TV work.

Nonetheless, a video game generally includes many of the same elements as movies, such as story lines, characters, dialogue, and visual and sound effects. But video games also feature puzzles, challenges, different levels, a user interface, an immersive world, and interactive features. The video game designer will have to work with a team of digital media artists as well as with teams of programmers tasked with handling the technical features. Video game designers also have extensive managerial duties, from setting the schedule to keeping under budget to working with the marketing department to overseeing testing of early versions.

A video game designer must have a solid understanding of both the creative and technical aspects of games. Artistic ability and mastery of design programs are less critical for this job than for many other positions in digital media, although the designer

should be familiar with basic computer programming and software tools. It's more essential that video game designers focus on narrative, scenarios, and mechanics of the game—the elements that will keep the user engaged.

Hand-drawn illustrations depict game pieces used in a chess mobile app game. In video game production, both artistic and technical aspects are essential to creating an appealing final product.

WEB DEVELOPER

A web developer creates websites. There are two aspects to building a website: the "front end" deals with design, and the "back end" refers to the technical construction. In some cases, the same person may be responsible for both the design and development, but often, the jobs are split between a web designer and the web developer. The web designer uses principles of graphic design to create the overall appearance and user experience of the site, which is laid out using design software.

While the web designer attends to the creative side, the web developer works on the technical backbone of the site.

TIPS FROM THE PROS

Steve Bowler, video game lead designer

- "I really enjoy the challenges of making games. It's one of the most mentally stimulating and rewarding fields I've ever worked in. It's also caused me the most anxiety and stress. We work very, very hard making the stuff you love.
- Learning to fail faster and approaching each problem as a unique challenge has helped a lot … In our business it feels like often there are no shortcuts, so personal experience and problem solving are often the best tools of the trade.
- Make games, write code, make art, every single day. If you're not doing it for your job, do it for yourself on your days off. You don't get to be the best by taking a single class or earning a degree or even landing a single job. You have to constantly challenge yourself."

(Source: Orin, Andy. "Career Spotlight: What I Do as a Game Designer." Life Hacker, May 6, 2015. http://lifehacker.com/career-spotlight-what-i-do-as-a-game-designer-1702637007.)

He or she writes the code using a variety of programming languages and software tools. The web developer launches the website and ensures that it runs smoothly from a technical standpoint, monitoring how it handles traffic and fixing any bugs that disrupt performance. Different types of sites provide individual challenges for web developers. A gaming website might require extensive interactive elements, while security measures would be more important for a retail website. As usage of mobile devices becomes ever more prevalent, web developers are being called on to create sites that function on screens of all sizes.

DIGITAL PHOTOGRAPHER

Digital photographs are everywhere on the internet and mobile platforms. In addition, the photos featured in print publications are often taken with digital cameras and edited with software before being printed.

Photographers can work across a variety of categories. Some photographers are fine artists whose work is displayed in galleries and museums. Photographers also work in the news business, documenting notable events and providing photos for stories related to sports, lifestyle, travel, and entertainment. A photographer may specialize in a particular type of photography, such as portraits, wildlife, aerial views, fashion, or science.

Photographers may work in a studio or on location, whether they're photographing an event, a shoot for an advertisement, or a nature landscape. Some photographers edit their photographs extensively using computer software. A photographer must be technically proficient in using equipment and artistically aware of factors such as composition, lighting, and choices about subject matter. Professional photographers who own their own studio must also develop good business skills. Photographers generally need to invest in quality equipment, beginning with a camera with various lenses appropriate for different situations.

WRITER

Writers are involved in every type of digital media, whether they're scripting the story for a movie, drafting advertising copy, writing the technical manuals consulted by digital media specialists, or reviewing movies, video games, and TV shows. A successful writer keeps the target audience and the medium in mind when writing for a project. A writer who is framing a story for a video game should be familiar with how games balance story elements with user participation. A screenwriter should be aware of proper formatting and legal considerations as well as have a flair for dialogue and the other elements of a screenplay. Copywriters for advertisers should be familiar with general principles of advertising and the specific requirements of the client.

Writers' work may also be showcased in online publications. Writers may submit a piece to an online publication or arrange for publication themselves. Online publications offer opportunities

for writers of all kinds, from science fiction novelists to free-lance journalists. There are also e-book publishing platforms that allow authors to publish and sell their books on their own.

A photographer sets up a group shot. Photographers who work in studios must pay attention to considerations such as lighting, lens choice, and composition of a portrait.

Digital media created a new publishing niche that didn't exist before the internet: the blog, short for "web log." Some bloggers have succeeded in making it a lucrative career, reaching a huge audience. Other blogs are published by media networks and specialize in a particular type of content, such as lifestyle or tech. Writers interested in blogging can start their own blog or submit content to an established blog.

DIGITAL MARKETING MANAGER

A company's marketing department (or a marketing agency hired by the company) identifies markets for the company's products or services and organizes promotional campaigns. Research and analysis are crucial to a campaign's success, enabling the marketing department to compete effectively against similar products or target a specific demographic group in the campaign. A successful marketing campaign raises consumer awareness and interest in a company's products. One popular element of a campaign is branding—creating a recognizable and favorable identity associated with the company and its products.

Digital media opened up a wealth of new possibilities for marketing managers. Today, online tools provide new ways of obtaining and analyzing marketing data. In implementing promotional strategies, marketing managers devise ways to steer traffic to their website. They take advantage of social media to engage the public and release digital content such as promotional videos, graphics, and text—tasks that might be assigned to a digital media specialist.

chapter 3

PREPARING FOR A DIGITAL MEDIA CAREER

I t's easy to get excited at the prospect of a career working in digital media. You might be inspired by some eye-popping examples of digital media handiwork found in various forms of entertainment, from the special effects in movies to the immersive realities created for video games to stunning 3D animation. Or maybe you've benefited from some of the practical applications of digital media, from educational tools to new developments in scientific research. If these spectacles and breakthroughs prompt you to start dreaming of ways that you could use digital media to create works of your own, you might consider pursuing a career in the field.

For high school students, the process starts by learning about the personal and educational requirements for jobs in digital media. You should take advantage of school courses and extracurricular opportunities related to the field and plan to continue formal study in college.

IS DIGITAL MEDIA FOR YOU?

Whether their medium of choice is animation, photographs, graphics, or the written word, digital media specialists feel the urge to create. Artistic talent and imagination are crucial for these careers, but technical expertise is essential, as well, to

Any job listing in fields related to digital media emphasizes the importance of good communication skills in a variety of settings, from social media updates to giving effective presentations.

transform concepts into reality. Anyone considering a career in digital media must be willing to dedicate time and effort to master the software used in the industry. You should also be enthusiastic about novel tech trends and breakthroughs—the tools and techniques used in digital media are constantly evolving, and you'll need to keep on learning to stay up to date.

Communication skills are crucial in the field of digital media. Many digital media specialists work as part of a team. Verbal and written skills are important in day-to-day work. Presentation skills can be critical in an industry that requires content to make a quick and enduring positive impression.

Digital media specialists should also be savvy about social media—and this astuteness goes beyond posting clever quips online. A successful social media strategy must attract and engage a target audience in a specific niche.

A job in digital media may involve juggling multiple projects with tight deadlines. To succeed, you must possess a strong work ethic, attention to detail, the ability to work under pressure, and good time-management skills.

PREPARING AT SCHOOL FOR A DIGITAL MEDIA CAREER

Students with a strong interest in digital media can take advantage of opportunities to gain relevant knowledge and experience while still in high school. The field of digital media requires both technical and creative skills. You should take a variety of computer classes even if you aren't planning on specializing in design or programming—digital literacy is crucial for most job descriptions. Courses in art, photography, and film, if available, can help you establish a background in a variety of different areas in digital media. English classes will help you improve communication skills.

Extracurricular activities can also help students prepare for a digital media career. Your school or community might offer activities directly related to digital media, such as a digital media club, a school newspaper, or amateur film production opportunities. General organizational and volunteer activities also provide opportunities to gain experience that may be valuable in the workplace, whether it's participating in a robotics competition, running for office in student government, doing volunteer work, or joining the debate team. Listing a summer job on your résumé will show that you're responsible and willing to work hard. Tech-savvy high school students might pursue employment that requires digital media experience or turn their expertise to entrepreneurship by offering their services to people in need of help with their

Many digital media professionals benefit from coursework related to art and photography, which can help an aspiring game designer or film editor gain proficiency in transforming ideas into visual depictions.

computers, mobile devices, or online presence.

Students who are in high school should also begin putting together a digital design portfolio, which is typically stored and displayed online. A portfolio is a showcase of your best work. In creating a digital portfolio, you should include a range of samples such as articles, videos, projects, graphics, photos, or web pages and present the selections in a way that will grab the viewer's attention. There are services online that can help users create a digital portfolio; ask a teacher or adviser for recommendations.

In addition, students should be aware of their digital footprint, the impression created by their online presence. Colleges and employers do check the social media presence and other online activities of prospective students or employees. To create a favorable impression, students should emphasize their academic and professional achievements and make sure that they use privacy settings to protect their personal information.

PLANNING FOR COLLEGE

Most jobs in digital media require at least a bachelor's degree, so you should anticipate attending a four-year college. Some schools offer majors in digital media, in which students study the theory and gain hands-on experience in various forms of digital art and graphic design. Students typically learn computer programming, website development, and the creation and production of various types of media, from graphics to special effects. But there are many different pathways toward a career in digital media. You might consider a highly specific major, such as video game design, interactive media, or animation, or a broader major, such as film, communications, computer programming, or art. Consider a minor or coursework in other relevant aspects of digital media that complement your major.

A teacher lectures during a computer programming class. It's essential that digital media professionals develop solid technical skills and stay up to date with the latest technological developments.

The cost of a college education can be quite daunting. Look for scholarships related to study in digital media. You can do research online and talk to your teachers or advisers about finding scholarships. Some scholarships are merit based, while others are need based or targeted toward specific demographic groups.

WORKING YOUR NETWORK

Most professionals working in digital media emphasize the importance of networking—maintaining contact and open communication with others in the field. Early on, your network will consist of professors, advisers, fellow students and alumni in your program of study, and former employers. Some new entrants in a field benefit from having a mentor who can offer guidance based on experience. Your family and friends may also offer support; professional and social circles can overlap in this era of social media. Your first job will give you the opportunity to impress your colleagues with your work performance. The quality of your work is your first priority, of course, but keep in mind that they'll be more likely to recommend you for future jobs if they enjoy working with you, too.

If you use your network effectively, you'll establish a solid professional reputation for yourself in the industry. As you gain experience, your network will expand to include colleagues and collaborators in related areas of the field. Make an effort to meet people in the industry through associations, organizations, and conferences. Your networking contacts will be able to offer advice, referrals, and leads on promising job openings as you begin to establish yourself in the field. Later on, you'll probably have a chance to reciprocate.

INTERNSHIPS

Internships are short-term trainee positions—often unpaid or low paying—for students and recent graduates. Many college students hunt for summer internships during the spring semester; new college graduates may complete a longer internship to prepare for regular employment. Some college and university programs in digital media require internships before a student can graduate. These programs offer course credit for the internships and can require a minimum number of clock hours of supervised work for each credit earned.

Internships can be a mutually beneficial arrangement for both the intern and employer. The intern gains valuable work experience, new skills, and professional contacts in the industry. During the course of an internship, an intern may learn valuable insights from a mentor—a supervisor or colleague willing to share advice, offer support, and write a letter of recommendation at some point later on. Sometimes, an internship can lead to a job offer at the company. In turn, the employer gets the talent, hard work, and enthusiasm of newcomers in the field.

Internships can be found through general career sites, direct listings on company

Internships provide students and recent graduates with hands-on experience in the work environment in their field and a valuable opportunity to get tips from savvy professionals.

websites, college career resources departments, and professional networking. Employers are likelier to pay attention to applications specifically tailored to the company's needs. If the listing calls for specific skills, such as software proficiency or project management experience, for example, be sure to emphasize your in-demand qualifications.

The best internships provide educational opportunities that give the interns a chance to find out if they're really a good fit for the field. Unfortunately, though, some internships exploit interns by assigning them menial tasks rather than hands-on job experience. Prospective interns should research companies before accepting an internship offer and learn about the US Department of Labor's guidelines for internship programs.

chapter 4

GETTING THE JOB

Finding the first job of your digital media career will require dedication, organization, networking, and thorough preparation. As you begin searching for your first job, you'll need to assess your short-term and long-term career goals. Research general trends in the industry and projections for growth. A wide range of companies hire digital media specialists, from the video game industry to software companies to advertising agencies. Once you've established a clear vision of your dream job, the next step is to check the job listings for entry-level positions in the field. Typically, you'll start out as a member of a team working behind the scenes on the production of videos, animations, games, or other projects. But to get hired, you'll have to convince the company that you're the best candidate for the job.

READING THE JOB LISTINGS

It's often said that during the job search, a job seeker should consider finding employment to be a job in itself. You should be organized, determined, and methodical as you take advantage of all the resources that could lead to landing a position.

If you begin a job search as a student or recent alumni, you might choose to start with a visit to your school's career resource center. You'll be able to view job listings and take advantage of services for job seekers, from résumé critiques to workshops on acing an interview. Some schools hold career fairs where you can meet with representatives from companies that are hiring. Your professors and fellow students may also be able to let you know about job openings in the field as well. You should also ask former professors, supervisors, or advisers for letters of recommendation to potential employers and check whether they would be willing to serve as references.

The internet offers a wealth of job listings, from huge general career sites to employment sections of big companies or professional organizations related to the field of digital media. Try using a variety of search terms and strategies. Instead of searching for "digital media jobs" on jobs sites, for example, look for "multimedia jobs" and other likely titles related to your specialization.

First-time job seekers might be unaware that many open positions are filled without even being listed. You may be able to gain access to some such jobs through connections and networking. As mentioned, academic contacts can be valuable; you can also reach out to colleagues from internships and past jobs. Look into professional associations or organizations related to your specialization. Business-oriented online social networking sites, such as LinkedIn, can help you search for

jobs and establish professional relationships with other users. Personal social networks, such as Facebook and Twitter, can be useful for maintaining connections with colleagues in your field, too. If you hope to land a job at a specific company, take

Events such as college career fairs provide a chance for students to learn about entry-level job openings and internships in their field directly from prospective employers.

the initiative to send that company an unsolicited résumé. If the hiring managers are impressed, they may get in touch or keep your résumé on file for when they have an opening.

POLISHING YOUR RÉSUMÉ

A résumé is a summary of a job applicant's work history and relevant qualifications for a job. It's a chance to introduce yourself to prospective employers and showcase your accomplishments ahead of a job interview.

All résumés include contact information and sections on education and work experience. Other possible headings include skills and qualifications, honors and achievements, certification and credentials, or volunteer service. A section on

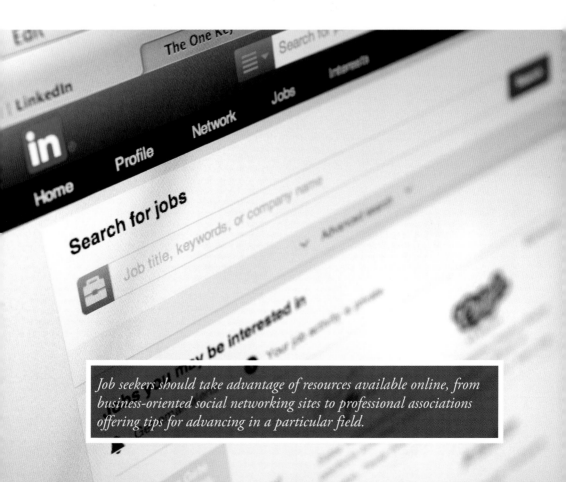

Job seekers should take advantage of resources available online, from business-oriented social networking sites to professional associations offering tips for advancing in a particular field.

technical knowledge may be relevant for many digital media specializations. You might choose to include hobbies and interests, but only if these are relevant to the job description. Some résumés include an objective at the beginning and references at the end.

You should start building your résumé while you're still in high school and update it regularly. If you lack work experience, emphasize your accomplishments achieved in various activities. Instead of merely listing that coursework in computer programming, elaborate by briefly describing a relevant class project that might impress a prospective employer. Instead of stating that you participated in volunteer activities, mention that you worked as part of a team to organize a fund-raiser.

When applying for a job, you should research the company and tailor your résumé to emphasize skills and accomplishments relevant to the position. Include keywords relevant to the job description that are likely to grab the employer's attention.

There are several different formats for résumés, and you should research the standard format for your field. Pay attention to any submission requirements in the job description; the employer may request that you either attach a résumé to an email or include the text in the body of the message. As a digital media specialist, you might consider creating an online digital résumé that includes graphics and multimedia elements.

Job seekers generally include a cover letter in a job application. A cover letter offers the opportunity to make the case that you're a great candidate for the job. Unlike a résumé, which serves primarily to convey information about your professional qualifications, a cover letter gives you a chance to demonstrate your communication skills and a sense of your personality— but be sure to maintain a professional tone. You shouldn't rehash the content of your résumé exactly, but you might choose to highlight a couple of your exceptional accomplishments in a cover letter.

KELSEY TAYLOR

8033 Orchard Lane • Waterloo, IA 50701
Home: (319) 932-5849 • Cell: (319) 895-3817 • kmtaylor@mac.com

OBJECTIVE

A position as a digital media specialist where I can use my creative and technical skills to promote a brand through social media presence.

EDUCATION

Waterloo High School, 2010
B.A., University of Iowa, 2014, Communications Studies

WORK EXPERIENCE

2014–Present
Dolent Technologies • **Social Media Specialist**
• Monitored and updated content on various social media platforms
• Worked as part of a team designing marketing campaigns across social media, web, email, press release, and video
• Researched innovative social media marketing concepts, strategy, and best practices

School Year 2013–2014
Teaching Assistant, Introduction to Communication • University of Iowa Department of Communication Studies

• Assisted the professor in preparing lectures
• Graded papers and examinations
• Led review sessions for examinations

Summer 2013
Social Marketing Intern • **Alten Media**
• Helped develop and implement online marketing campaigns
• Managed Alten Media's social media presence and engaged with customers online
• Strategized corporate re-branding on social media platforms

2013–Present
• Contributor to a music-related blog
• Authored reviews of local live concerts
• Updated content and designed new layout of blog

SKILLS

• Excellent written, verbal, and social media communication skills
• Good at multitasking and time management
• Superior technical troubleshooting skills
• Three years of Spanish language classes

Web Tools
• Adobe Creative Suite
• Microsoft Office Suite
• FileMaker Pro
• Google AdWords
• WordPress

References available upon request

This is an example of a résumé for a digital media specialist position. An effective résumé conveys the candidate's skills and accomplishments in addition to work history.

ACING THE INTERVIEW

If your résumé impresses a potential employer, the next step is a job interview. Sometimes, companies screen applicants by arranging an initial phone interview. This call is your chance to convince the interviewer that you are excited and well qualified for the job.

You should be well prepared for both the phone interview and the in-person interview. Research the company, and review the requirements of the position. Rehearse answers for a range of questions that are likely to arise, and remember that the interviewer will be assessing your potential as an employee as well as your qualifications. Expect open-ended questions such as "Tell me about yourself" or "Where do you see yourself in five years?" Give answers that emphasize your professionalism and your enthusiasm for the industry. Practice talking about

Be sure to demonstrate a positive attitude during a job interview to show the employer that you'd be a good person to work with on a day-to-day basis.

the technical details of the job; employers appreciate candidates with the communication skills to convey complex aspects of the field in terms that both laymen and other experts can easily grasp.

Focus on ways that you can make a great first impression. Dress for success in professional attire, and try to project a positive, confident attitude. If you're reluctant by nature to boast about your accomplishments, remind yourself that this interview is your chance to showcase the abilities and experience that you can bring to the job. You don't want to come off as a braggart, but you shouldn't undersell yourself, either. The internet and general career guidance books can provide specific tips for acing an interview.

You should follow up an interview with a thank-you note or email. If you don't hear back from the interviewers, wait at least a week or two before making a follow-up call about the status of the hiring process for the job.

chapter 5

WORKING FREELANCE

Today, more and more Americans work in the sector sometimes called the gig economy. Instead of relying on a single full-time job, they support themselves through short-term or contract employment. According to *Fast Company*, over a third of the workforce participates in freelancing, meaning that they are self-employed and perform work on a per-project basis for companies. Today, computers and the internet provide the means for many workers to do their job in any place or at any time. They aren't tied to a specific workplace. Because the internet also facilitates professional networking, it's easier than ever before to succeed as a freelancer.

Many professionals in the field of digital media work freelance. According to the BLS, over half of all multimedia artists and animators are self-employed. Likewise, many writers and photographers work freelance, and some graphic designers and web developers also consider freelancing an attractive option. Typically, digital media workers contract with a client to complete a specific project or service, such as setting up a website, creating graphics for an advertising campaign, or writing an article.

Some digital media specialists plan out a strategy to succeed as a freelancer. Others take a few contract jobs to support themselves while looking for work and fall into a pattern of freelancing almost by chance. Not all freelancers support themselves solely from contract gigs. Some have full-time or part-time jobs and do freelance work on the side. Many freelancers work at home, but some rent office space for their business dealings.

ADVANTAGES AND DISADVANTAGES TO FREELANCING

If you're considering establishing yourself as a freelance digital media specialist, you should begin by weighing whether freelancing is right for you. You must be self-motivated to succeed as a freelancer. You won't have a supervisor checking on your progress or offering feedback—you have to hold yourself accountable for your own progress. You also must possess superior time management skills. You'll not only have to keep track of deadlines for multiple projects but also have to balance work and home life. In addition, freelancing requires skills and abilities that go beyond professional qualifications. Freelancing is a business. If you work for a large company,

Some freelancers establish a home office that they use exclusively for work. Setting regular office hours is one way to maintain good work habits and stay productive.

you're supported by departments such as administrative, accounting, customer service, sales, marketing, advertising, and legal. As a freelancer, you have to attend to all those aspects on your own.

There are many advantages to working as a freelancer. Many freelancers appreciate the flexibility and freedom. They set their own schedules, make their own decisions, and don't have to answer to a boss. Many digital media freelancers can work any place that they can take their computer. Because they can choose their clients and jobs, freelancers often have more variety in their work than regular employees who spend working hours on the same tasks.

There are also drawbacks to freelancing. Working as a freelancer can provide less security than a full-time job with a steady income. Work opportunities are sometimes irregular, and freelancers should be able to cope with the possibility of inconsistency and instability in their financial situation. Freelancers sometimes struggle to find clients, while at other times, they might find themselves overloaded with projects. Employers don't always treat freelancers well—sometimes, freelancers have to fight just to get paid for their work. Finally, freelancers lack the benefits of full-time employment, such as health insurance, retirement plans, paid vacation or sick time, or the promise of unemployment compensation if they lose their job.

MAKING CONNECTIONS

For many freelancers, finding clients is the most challenging part of the job. Just as when you look for a full-time job, you need to work your network. Stay in touch with former classmates, teachers, and colleagues. If a client is satisfied with your job, ask him or her to recommend you if another project becomes available. A good reputation is a valuable asset for a freelancer. Establish a

RUNNING YOUR OWN BUSINESS

A freelancer essentially runs a one-person business. Freelancers have to attend to certain practical factors that regular hired employees don't have to worry about. A few examples are as follows:

- A business plan—set goals and strategies.
- A business license—check if you need one in your city or state.
- Dealing with taxes—find out which forms you will need to file. In addition, freelancers may have to make quarterly payments.
- Buying insurance—sign up for health, life, and other types of insurance.
- Paperwork—learn about contracts, invoices, expense records, and other legal or bureaucratic requirements.
- Getting a loan—obtain a business loan to start a business or buy equipment.

Not every freelancer has to take all these considerations into account—one of the advantages to freelancing is the freedom to try different approaches to the business side of the work.

professional social media presence to publicize your services, as well as a business website with a portfolio and profile pages on sites of relevant professional associations. Look into joining websites that offer freelancer services to clients—they often offer low pay and impose strict conditions on workers, but they can provide valuable experience and contacts in the industry, especially if you're just starting out. Identify potential clients and contact them with a sales pitch, particularly if you're already aware that a company hires freelancers in your field.

You'll gain confidence in dealing with clients as you become more experienced working as your own agent. Early on, you will probably grapple with the issue of how much to charge for a job. You'll have to learn how to negotiate for reasonable pay

A freelancer must be ready to interact with different types of clients. Share your digital portfolio with prospective employers so that they can see the range of work and experience that you can provide.

rates from clients. Some freelancers recommend that to improve your prospects, you should charge higher rates for new clients than for established clients.

FINDING YOUR NICHE

To attract clients, consider specializing in a particular area of the digital media business. A graphic designer might establish a reputation for a certain advertising niche. A photographer might concentrate in photographing certain types of events, or an animator might focus on projects for mobile apps.

Instead of scrambling to fill any available job as a jack-of-all-trades, try to pick projects in which you believe that you can distinguish yourself from other freelancers. When companies hire a freelancer for a project, they evaluate the portfolio, qualifications, and experience of applicants for the job. They consider whether the freelancer has the passion and the flair that they're looking for—don't lose sight of the fact that digital media jobs are often creative endeavors that require imagination and an eye for visual effectiveness. As you acquire skills and a solid reputation, companies may make you their first contact for certain types of projects.

Freelancers must make an effort to be current on trends and developments in their industry. They may opt to utilize educational resources online or attend tech events, for example.

Make sure that you stay abreast of developments in your industry, including both technical advances and emerging business trends. Innovative technology is constantly expanding the possibilities in areas such as special effects, animation, and web design. In the recent past, freelancers who appreciated the potential of new business trends such as blogs, mobile technology, and social media were able to exploit their promise ahead of colleagues in the field. You should be willing to adapt to emerging technology—keep an eye open for the next big thing that might prove advantageous in your freelancing career.

chapter 6

LONG-TERM LEARNING AND ADVANCEMENT

A first job is sometimes described as a foot in the door of an industry or a stepping-stone to positions with more responsibility that require on-the-job experience and offer better pay. Once you've landed a job in digital media, you'll probably start out doing some of the most basic tasks of anyone on your team. Your job description might be that of a technician or assistant. A first job is a learning experience, and you'll get a chance to gain expertise and prove your aptitude with hands-on work. Once you've gained confidence, you might discover that you have natural abilities in a certain area or that you're interested in expanding your skill set in a particular niche. Keep an open mind, and be willing to learn constantly about the work going on around you—you'll benefit from gaining an understanding of the responsibilities that your colleagues and collaborators carry out during a project.

LOOKING TO THE FUTURE

Even as you establish yourself in a digital media job, you might occasionally ask yourself "What's next?" If you're in a

As digital media specialists gain experience and expertise, they may take on more responsibilities or move up to a supervisory role.

specialized subfield within digital media, you might find yourself drawn toward work in related areas. A 3D artist may consider trying animation, or a graphic designer working in web design might decide to try out a video game project. A writer might try freelance editing. Most people who are employed in creative areas of digital media also work on their own projects independently. Don't overlook unexpected opportunities, but weigh the benefits and drawbacks carefully if you think a project could be a risky prospect.

There's no single ladder for advancement in digital media; the field is made up of many different career paths that each have different potentials for the future. A digital media specialist might be promoted to a position with more supervisory responsibilities. Instead of updating social media accounts and editing promotional clips, you'll be giving directions to the people in charge of those types of tasks. In addition, expertise in digital media can

A DAY IN THE LIFE OF A FRONT-END WEB DEVELOPER

This description of the everyday responsibilities of a web developer highlights the importance of staying abreast of the latest technological trends in the industry.

"Always keeping up with design and code trends, it is the front-end specialist who keeps a website's experience on the cutting edge.

As a Front End Developer, it'll be your job to make websites awesome!

How you'll spend your day:

• Collaborating with clients, content creators, designers, back end developers and management
• Interpreting designers visions …
• Combining the work of designers and back end developers …
• Testing … optimizing … and fixing websites …
• Researching design and coding trends to keep websites cutting edge …

One of the major demands of a front-end developer is staying on top of design and code trends to always present the most relevant, inviting, and engaging visual experience and interaction for users."

(Source: Zomick, Brad. "Life of a Front-End Web Developer." SkilledUp, April 24, 2014. http://www.skilledup.com/articles/life-front-end-web-developer-infographic.)

be valuable in other settings. If a digital media specialist decides to change careers, skills acquired as a digital media specialist can be applied to jobs in education, government, public relations, cultural institutions such as museums, and many other fields that benefit from cultivating a positive image through digital media.

If you work within a specialized area of digital media, pay attention to the supervisory structure of your workplace in assessing your career goals. Typically, you might start out as a technician, artist, editor, apprentice, or assistant on a team, then be assigned to more important roles once you've proven your abilities. A junior programmer might be promoted to lead programmer, for example. Then you might eventually become head of your division and finally director or producer of your department. A graphic art technician for a video game, for example, might in time become a full graphic designer and finally take on a wider range of responsibilities as art director. A successful and ambitious film editor might advance to directing movies; the acclaimed director Martin Scorsese, for example, started out as a film editor.

KEEPING UP TO DATE

A commitment to lifelong learning and keeping up with new technology is essential for a career in digital media. In many areas of digital media, technology is continually evolving and becoming more advanced. Devices and programs are constantly being released that incorporate new and updated features and capabilities. For every innovation that's introduced—from social media to 3D to virtual reality and beyond—specialists in various fields of digital media will assess whether or not the technology will be widely adopted and appreciated. Some novel products prove to be fads that

Students test a game in a college's virtual reality lab. Digital media specialists must keep abreast of cutting-edge technology and be able to decide whether or not it should be adopted by their employers.

fizzle, but others will become popular and enduring. Early adopters will be well positioned for future work with these technologies. Likewise, specialists who work in marketing or advertising will need to constantly track current social trends to keep up to date on the type of campaigns that will engage the public.

On a more practical level, to advance and compete effectively, you must keep up with the latest tools of the trade. You might consider completing certification in software programs that are prevalent in your specialization. If your work involves programming or design, you could periodically sign up for online refresher courses to stay on top of current trends and new developments.

Earning a master's degree in digital media, communications, business, or other relevant subject can provide the opportunity to obtain valuable new skills and make

Digital media specialists need to acquire new skills to continue to be competitive in their field. A web designer, for example, should be aware of popular new concepts or innovative coding tools.

a candidate for a position stand out from competition in the field, particularly in terms of management potential. You'll find yourself confronting unexpected new challenges if you begin to take on more managerial tasks. Managers have to provide leadership, both in broad respects, such as being able to motivate their team to perform their best, and in specific settings, such as being effective in leading a meeting. You'll have to learn how to put together a team and delegate responsibility. In return for your increased commitment, you'll feel an even greater sense of satisfaction upon successful completion of a project.

glossary

animation The process of creating the appearance of movement using a sequence of images.

bachelor's degree The undergraduate degree obtained after completing a four-year college program.

blog Short for "web log," a website, often personal or informal in nature, in which a person or group of people regularly add updates. Also, to post material to a blog.

certification The awarding of a certificate or license upon completion of a course of study or passing of an exam.

credential Proof, usually written, that demonstrates someone's identity, authority, or qualifications.

digital media Encoded electronic data that is read and transmitted by computers and other devices.

freelancer A person who works on specific projects, often on a contract basis for multiple clients, rather than as a long-term employee of a company.

immersive Giving a user the impression that he or she is actually experiencing a setting created by digital media.

innovation The introduction of a new product, technology, idea, and so forth.

interactive Allowing two-way communication between a human and a computer or other system.

intern A trainee or low-level assistant, especially one who takes employment to gain practical experience.

license Official permission from the government or other authority, such as to practice a trade.

management The executives or administrators who direct and operate a business or organization.

marketing The process of promoting a product or service to potential buyers.

master's degree An advanced degree obtained after completing a one- or two-year graduate program.

multimedia Describing a program, project, or piece of art that incorporates elements from any combination of text, images, sound, animation, or video.

network To maintain communication with a group of people, especially to exchange information about professional opportunities.

portfolio A representative sampling of work that displays someone's accomplishments or abilities.

publicize To promote, advertise, or bring to wide public notice.

reference Someone providing a statement of professional qualifications; also, the statement itself.

résumé A summary of one's professional qualifications and work experience.

Academy of Interactive Arts and Sciences
11175 Santa Monica Boulevard, Fourth Floor
Los Angeles, CA 90025
(310) 484-2560
Website: http://www.interactive.org
Facebook: @AcademyofInteractiveArtsandSciences
Twitter: @Official_AIAS
The mission of the Academy of Interactive Arts and Sciences
is to promote and advance the worldwide interactive
entertainment community; recognize outstanding achievements in the interactive arts and sciences; host an annual
awards show, the D.I.C.E. Awards; and enhance awareness
of the interactive art form.

Canadian Media Producers Association (CMPA)
160 John Street, 5th Floor
Toronto, ON M5V 2E5
Canada
(416) 304-0280
Website: http://cmpa.ca
Facebook: @theCMPA
Twitter: @the_cmpa
The CMPA is a Canadian trade association for independent
producers, representing companies engaged in the devel-
opment, production, and distribution of English-language
television programs, feature films, and digital media.

CGSociety
+61 8 8463 1866
Website: http://www.cgsociety.org

Facebook: @cgsociety
Twitter: @cgsociety
The CGSociety is a global organization for creative digital artists that supports artists at every level by offering a range
of services to connect, inform, educate, and promote digital artists worldwide.

Entertainment Software Association (ESA)
601 Massachusetts Avenue NW, Suite 300
Washington, DC 20001
Website: http://www.theesa.com
Facebook: @TheEntertainmentSoftwareAssociation
Twitter: @RichatESA
The ESA is the association dedicated to serving the business
and public affairs needs of companies that publish com-
puter and video games for video game consoles, handheld
devices, personal computers, and the internet.

International Alliance of Theatrical Stage Employees, Moving
Picture Technicians, Artists and Allied Crafts of the Unit-
ed States, Its Territories and Canada (IATSE)
207 West Twenty-Fifth Street, Fourth Floor
New York, NY 10001
(212) 730-1770
Website: http://www.iatse.net
Facebook: @iatse
Twitter: @iatse

IATSE Canadian Office
22 St. Joseph Street
Toronto, ON M4Y 1J9
Canada
(416) 362-3569
The IATSE is a union representing members in all forms of

live theater, motion picture and television production, trade shows and exhibitions, television broadcasting, and concerts as well as the equipment and construction shops that support all these areas of the entertainment industry.

International Game Developers Association (IGDA)
19 Mantua Road
Mt. Royal, NJ 08061
Website: http://www.igda.org
Facebook: @IGDA.org
Twitter: @IGDA
IGDA is a nonprofit membership organization serving all individuals from all fields of game development, focusing on advocacy, networking, professional development, and international reach.

WEBSITES

Because of the changing nature of internet links, Rosen Publishing has developed an online list of websites related to the subject of this book. This site is updated regularly. Please use this link to access the list:

http://www.rosenlinks.com/ECAR/Digital

for further reading

Bolles, Richard N. *What Color Is Your Parachute? A Practical Manual for Job-Hunters and Career-Changers.* Rev. ed. Berkeley, CA: Ten Speed Press, 2017.

DeCarlo, Laura. *Resumes for Dummies.* Hoboken, NJ: John Wiley & Sons, Inc., 2015.

Fry, Ronald W. *101 Great Answers to the Toughest Interview Questions.* Wayne, NJ: Career Press, 2016.

Furgang, Adam. *Internship and Volunteer Opportunities for TV and Movie Buffs* (Foot in the Door). New York: Rosen Publishing, 2013.

Furgang, Kathy. *Careers in Digital Animation* (Careers in Computer Technology). New York: Rosen Publishing, 2014.

Gregory, Josh. *Animation: From Concept to Consumer* (Calling All Innovators). New York: Children's Press, 2015.

Hand, Carol. *Getting Paid to Produce Videos* (Turning Your Tech Hobbies into a Career). New York: Rosen Publishing, 2017.

Kennedy, Sam R. *How to Become a Video Game Artist.* New York: Watson-Guptill Publications, 2013.

Klein, Rebecca T. *Career Building Through Using Digital Publishing Tools* (Digital Career Building). New York: Rosen Publishing, 2014.

Nagle, Jeanne. *Careers in Internet Advertising and Marketing* (Careers in Computer Technology). New York: Rosen Publishing, 2014.

Nichols, Susan. *Cool Careers Without College for People Who Love Tech* (Cool Careers Without College). New York: Rosen Publishing, 2017.

Pollak, Lindsey. *Getting from College to Career: Your Essential Guide to Succeeding in the Real World.* Rev. ed. New York: Harper Business, 2012.

Ryan, Peter K. *Careers in Electronic Publishing* (Careers in Computer Technology). New York: Rosen Publishing, 2014.

Suen, Anastasia. *Internship and Volunteer Opportunities for People Who Love All Things Digital* (Foot in the Door). New York: Rosen Publishing, 2013.

Yate, Martin. *Knock 'em Dead: Secrets and Strategies for First-Time Job Seekers.* 12th ed. Avon, MA: Adams Media, 2013.

bibliography

The Art Career Project. "How to Become a Film Editor." 2014. Retrieved March 9, 2017. http://www .theartcareerproject.com/become-film-editor.

Carroll, Brian. *Writing for Digital Media*. New York, NY: Routledge, 2010.

Creative Uncut Video Game Art and Design. "How to Be a Video Game Designer or Artist." Retrieved March 7, 2017. http://www.creativeuncut.com/how-to-be -a-video-game-designer.html.

Dishman, Lydia. "How the Gig Economy Will Change in 2017." Fast Company, January 5, 2017. https://www .fastcompany.com/3066905/the-future-of-work/how -the-gig-economy-will-change-in-2017.

Duermyer, Randy. "What Is a Freelancer and What Is Free- lancing?" The Balance, February 06, 2017. https:// www.thebalance.com/what-is-freelancing-1794415.

Enelow, Wendy S., and Louise M. Kursmark. *Expert Re- sumes for Computer and Web Jobs*. 3rd ed. Indianapolis, IN: JIST Works, 2011.

Field, Shelly. *Career Coach: Managing Your Career in the Computer Industry.* New York, NY: Ferguson, 2009.

Heller, Steven, and David Womack. *Becoming a Digital Designer: A Guide to Careers in Web, Video, Broadcast, Game + Animation Design*. Hoboken, NJ: John Wiley & Sons, Inc., 2008.

Milton, Dell. "Dreamworks Animator Rebecca Perez." Ani- mation Arena. Retrieved March 9, 2017. http://www. animationarena.com/dreamworks-animator -rebecca-perez.html.

Moran, Matthew. *Building Your I.T. Career: A Complete Toolkit for a Dynamic Career in Any Economy.* 2nd ed. Indianapolis, IN: Pearson, 2013.

Orin, Andy. "Career Spotlight: What I Do as a Game Designer." Lifehacker, May 6, 2015. http://lifehacker.com /career-spotlight-what-i-do-as-a-game-designer -1702637007.

Taylor, Allan, and James Robert Parish. *Career Opportunities in the Internet, Video Games, and Multimedia.* New York, NY: Checkmark Books, 2007.

Tortorella, Neil. *Starting Your Career as a Freelance Web Designer.* New York, NY: Allworth Press, 2011.

US Department of Labor, Bureau of Labor Statistics. "Advertising, Promotions, and Marketing Managers." *Occupational Outlook Handbook*, December 17, 2015. https://www.bls.gov/ooh.

Yager, Fred, and Jan Yager. *Career Opportunities in the Film Industry.* 2nd ed. New York, NY: Checkmark Books, 2009.

Yate, Martin John. *Knock 'em Dead: The Ultimate Job Search Guide 2017.* Avon, MA: Adams Media, 2016.

Young, Antony. *Brand Media Strategy: Integrated Communications Planning in the Digital Era.* 2nd ed. New York, NY: Palgrave Macmillan, 2014.

Zomick, Brad. "Life of a Front-End Web Developer." SkilledUp, April 24, 2014. http://www.skilledup.com /articles/life-front-end-web-developer-infographic.

index

ABOUT THE AUTHOR

Corona Brezina is an author who has written several career-related books for young adults. Some of her previous titles that have focused on topics related to technology and in-demand careers include *Marc Andreessen* (Tech Pioneers); *Sergey Brin, Larry Page, Eric Schmidt, and Google* (Internet Biographies); *Top STEM Careers in Math* (Cutting-Edge STEM Careers), and *Careers in Nanotechnology* (Cutting-Edge Careers). She lives in Chicago, Illinois.

PHOTO CREDITS:

Cover, p. 1 (figure) Aaron Amat/Shutterstock.com; cover, p. 1 (background) Billion Photos/Shutterstock.com; pp. 4–5 Denys Prykhodov/Shutterstock.com; p. 8 dennizn/Shutterstock.com; pp. 10–11, 44–45, 64 © AP Images; p. 14 Bloomberg/Getty Images; pp. 16–17 Syda Productions/Shutterstock.com; pp. 22–23 Vintage Tone/Shutterstock.com; pp. 24–25 ymgerman/Shutterstock.com; pp. 26–27 Sander Koning/AFP/Getty Images; pp. 30–31 omgimages/iStock/Thinkstock; pp. 34–35 Hero Images/Getty Images; pp. 38–39 Akron Beacon Journal/Tribune News Service/Getty Images; pp. 40–41 Thomas Barwick/Taxi/Getty Images; pp. 50–51 Christian Science Monitor/Getty Images; pp. 54–55 sturti/E+/Getty Images; pp. 58–59 Richard Levine/Corbis News/Getty Images; pp. 61, 62–63 dotshock/Shutterstock.com; p. 67 JGalione/E+/Getty Images.

Design: Matt Cauli; Layout: Tahara Anderson; Senior Editor: Kathy Kuhtz Campbell; Photo Research: Karen Huang